THE LITTLE BOOK OF
THE ROLLING
STONES

THIS IS A CARLTON BOOK

Published by Carlton Books Ltd
20 Mortimer Street
London W1T 3JW

Text copyright © 2019 Carlton Books Ltd
Design copyright © 2019 Carlton Books Ltd

ISBN 978-1-78739-254-0

Editorial: Ross Hamilton
Design: Russell Knowles, Luana Gobo
Production: Yael Steinitz

A CIP catalogue for this book is available from the British Library

Printed in Dubai

10 9 8 7 6 5 4 3 2 1

Jacket cover photographs: Getty Images

THE LITTLE BOOK OF

THE ROLLING STONES

WISDOM AND WIT FROM
ROCK 'N' ROLL LEGENDS

CARLTON
BOOKS

CONTENTS

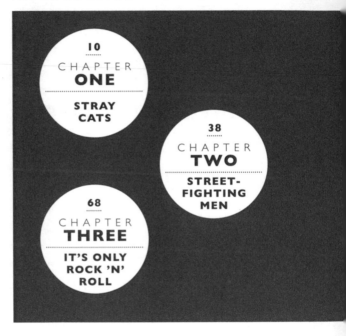

INTRODUCTION

It may only be rock and roll, but, when it comes to the Rolling Stones, nobody does it better. For more than five decades, this band of noisy blues hounds from London have shown the world what it means to be cool just by plugging in. Messrs Jagger, Richards, Stewart, Taylor, Jones, Watts, Wyman, Wood and – because you can do more time for murder, current bass player, Daryl Jones – may now be ridiculed as the band of rebels that refuse to retire, but that cannot diminish the truth: they are the greatest rock and rollers in the history of popular music.

The Rolling Stones first debuted on the soon-to-be swingin' London music scene in 1962, as the wild, loud and promiscuous "anti-Beatles", the pervy purveyors of butch blues and sweaty R&B, punch-drunk on the inspiration of their influences, a group who would go all night long most every night.

But they are also much more *than* just that reputation. The Stones are the band that continue to soundtrack popular culture's most recent centuries, merely by placing their sticky fingers on instruments and getting started up. As the years and tears have gone by, the Stones have continued to roll without gathering much moss. They are still discussed in the present tense with an ear-deafening reverence that just about equals the Beatles. One day, naturally, all we'll have of the Stones is their legacy of music, lyrics and wisdom. That and Keith Richards. Because, obviously, he's going to outlive us all.

CHAPTER

ONE

STRAY
CATS

66

I see a good little rock 'n' roll band – not as good as the Beatles, but good. **99**

Paul McCartney,
on the Rolling Stones

―――――――――――――――――――――

"

I knew what I was looking at. It was sex. And I was just ahead of the pack. **"**

Andrew Oldham, 1984

―――――――――――――――――――――

"

In the early days, we only played covers. The first album was all covers. I remember having this discussion, well, what are we going to do. We can't make a second album of covers. We already knew we'd come to the wall there. **"**

Mick Jagger

"

Every little moment hanging around, Keith and I used to be sitting with guitars, trying to write songs. We wrote songs all the time. We were constantly coming up with ideas. We started writing songs that were reflective of the time we were living in and that struck a chord with our audience. **"**

Mick Jagger

“

My father was furious with me, absolutely furious. I'm sure he wouldn't have been so mad if I'd have volunteered to join the army. Anything but this. He couldn't believe it. I agree with him: it wasn't a viable career opportunity. It was totally stupid. **”**

Mick Jagger,
on dropping out of college to form the band

"

Our reputation and image as the Bad Boys came later, completely there, accidentally. [...] Andrew Oldham never did engineer it. He simply exploited it exhaustively.

Bill Wyman, 1972

"

"

We were the first pop group to break away from the whole Cliff Richard thing where the bands did little dance steps, wore identical uniforms and had snappy patter.

Bill Wyman, 1972

_____

"

I'd rather be dead than singing
'Satisfaction' when I'm 45. "

Mick Jagger

_____

“

Everyone talks about rock these days; the problem is they forget about the roll.

”

Keith Richards

"

Mick is better with Keith Richards than he is with any other guitar players. I mean even a technically better guitar player – he's better with Keith. **"**

Charlie Watts

66

When Stu was playing, the band
swung a lot harder than when
he wasn't. **99**

Mick Jagger, on Ian Stewart

"

We wouldn't go on stage until Stu said, 'OK, you shower of shits, you're on.'

"

Bill Wyman, on Ian Stewart

66

You're not honestly asking that question, are you? I can't possibly answer that. **99**

Mick Jagger,
when asked if he had any regrets, 2011

"

I felt I was finally home.

,,

Ronnie Wood,
when he became a fully fledged member, 2011

"

Charlie hates fame. Charlie's perfect world would to be in the Rolling Stones but except nobody gives a shit who you are.

"

Keith Richards,
on Charlie Watts, 2012

"

It doesn't really change, actually. I think the Rolling Stones have gotten a lot better. An awful lot better, I think. A lot of people don't, but I think they have, and to me that's gratifying. It's worth it.

Charlie Watts

"

"

I'm quite happy to stay in the back there with the drums, where I belong. **"**

Bill Wyman

"

The Beatles looked like they were in show business, and that was the important thing. And the important thing for the Rolling Stones was to look as if they were not. **"**

Andrew Oldham, 2013

"

I told them who they were, and they became it. **"**

Andrew Oldham, 2013

"

Ian Stewart [Stu] was the one guy we tried to please. We wanted his approval when we were writing or rehearsing a song. **"**

Mick Jagger

"

Ian Stewart, I'm still working for him. To me, the Rolling Stones is his band. **"**

Keith Richards

"

I don't play minor chords. When I'm playing on stage with the Stones and a minor chord comes along, I lift me hands in protest. "

Ian Stewart

"

The Stones are a different kind of group. I realized that when I joined them. It's not really so much their musical ability, it's just they have a certain kind of style and attitude which is unique. **"**

Mick Taylor

"

You're always frustrated, you don't have the chance to do a song on the album, like the Beatles did with Ringo and George, or like Led Zeppelin, where everybody was given a chance to contribute. There never is a chance with the Stones.

"

Bill Wyman

"

What is a Rolling Stone? It's someone that is not settled. Like a pirate, a gypsy. Someone who likes to travel, voyage, an adventurer.

Charlie Watts, 2012

"

Writing songs is a great thing. It's like a jigsaw puzzle and a kaleidoscope put together; except, it's all done through the ears. And on that I would say Mick and I are probably very much on the same groove.

"

Keith Richards, 2012

CHAPTER

TWO

STREET-
FIGHTING
MEN

❝

It started, man, on the first tour. Halfway through it, things started to get crazy. **❞**

Keith Richards

"

In London [in the '60s], all kinds of shit was hitting the fan and, of course, we joined in. **"**

Keith Richards

66

My ultimate aim in life is that to be a pop star. I enjoy it, with reservations. But, I'm not really sort of satisfied, either artistically or personally. **99**

Brian Jones

"

Let's face it, the future as a Rolling Stone is very uncertain. **"**

Brian Jones

"

I don't think anyone can come between Mick and Keith — they're family. You can only go so far, and then you hit an invisible wall. They don't want anyone in there.

Charlie Watts

"

"

The whirlwind, the hurricane, the tornado of the – just being caught up in the band and the highs of the dope and the drink – my feet never really touched the ground for many years.

"

Ronnie Wood, 2012

"

The whole thing was out of control.
I mean, all normality and control
had gone. There was no – nothing.

Mick Jagger,
on the Altamont show

"

"

You talk about Rolling Stones, you know, it was an unstoppable momentum going on. And in a way, you were swept along with it. It's not as if you were particularly in control of it. Or, any of us were.

Keith Richards, 2012

"

❝

There was absolutely nothing wrong with him that a little extra love and understanding couldn't have cured. **❞**

George Harrison on Brian Jones

"

To me, Charlie Watts is the foundation of it all, because that's what I work off of, and we've been doing it all our lives. **"**

Keith Richards, 2008

"

That's all bullshit. Bullshit. I put that out because I was gonna have to clean up from all the dope. There's nothing like legend. **"**

Keith Richards,
on rumours of his blood transfusions, 2008

"

No, darling. Once you've sniffed it, you've sniffed it. **"**

Keith Richards,
when asked if he missed the drugs

"

I started off thinking about what being a performer meant when I was about 16. I hope I'm not being immodest, but I realized I would go out and do it, and the more people seemed to like it, the more I seemed to do stupid things and dance. You sort of realize that's your fate and you develop it.

"

Mick Jagger, 2011

___

"

I've never been enamoured of rock 'n' roll. It's never impressed me that much. **"**

Charlie Watts, 2011

___

"

Why would you want to be anything else if you're Mick Jagger? **"**

Keith Richards

"

The Stones in a club is still the ultimate rush. **"**

Keith Richards

66

We always have this moment of hesitation where we don't know if Keith's going to get the intro right.

Ronnie Wood, 2010

99

"

Brian had so many hang-ups he didn't know where to hang himself… so he drowned himself.

Keith Richards

"

I do what I do. Don't try this at home. **"**

Keith Richards

"

Rock and Roll: music for the neck downwards.

"

Keith Richards

"

As far as I'm concerned personally, and the boys in the band, if you're on stage with us, you're a Rolling Stone, and that's all there is to it.

Keith Richards,
on Daryl Jones, 2016

"

Ian Stewart was the glue that held the whole thing together. **"**

Keith Richards

66

I hate leaving home. I love what I do,
but I'd love to go home every night.

Charlie Watts

"

We lived and breathed the songs, Keith and I. Morning, noon and night and when we slept, which was very rare. Very rare! And we'd live and breathe other influences, whether it would be Mozart or Marley.

Ronnie Wood

"

I think between Mick, Brian and me, we had a feeling that the idea to put a band together that was a little less show-business was exactly at the right time. The show-biz angle was just boring to us. **"**

Keith Richards

66

Fitting into their mould was easy for me. I found the compatibility with playing, the whole lifestyle, the humour, the camaraderie. 99

Ronnie Wood,
on joining the band, 2012

66

In a way, the Stones saved me; because one thing that was more important than smack was the band.

Keith Richards

"

You just don't fuck with the Stones,
you know. **"**

Keith Richards

CHAPTER

THREE

IT'S ONLY
ROCK 'N' ROLL

66

He taught all the rest of us.

**David Bowie,
on Mick Jagger**

"

I thought rock and roll was an unassailable outlet for some pure and natural expression of rebellion. It used to be the one channel you could take without ever having to kiss ass, you know? "

Keith Richards

――――――――――――――――

"

Anything you throw yourself into,
you better get yourself out of.

Keith Richards

――――――――――――――――

"

We just got fed up with each other. You've got a relationship with musicians that depends on what you produce together. But when you don't produce, you get bad reactions – bands break up. "

Mick Jagger,
on Keith

"
We can't even get divorced.
I wanted to kill him.
"

Keith Richards, on Mick

"

It's never bothered me if the Rolling Stones stopped tomorrow.

Charlie Watts, 2011

"

"

I don't get paid for some of the biggest-selling records of all time. Frankly, I was ripped off. You get cynical about the music business and it stops you playing.

Mick Taylor 1997

"

"

Rock and roll has probably given more than it's taken. **"**

Charlie Watts

"

When they'd hit the big time, I was still at school. My sister was a big Stones fan. She always reminds me of when she would put 'Little Red Rooster' on and I'd say, 'Turn that rubbish off and put *Revolver* on.'

Mick Taylor

"

" We took his one thing away, which was being in a band. **"**

Charlie Watts,
about Brian Jones, 1989

" Keith and I took drugs… But, Brian took too many drugs of the wrong kind and he wasn't functioning as a musician. I don't think he was that interested in contributing to the Rolling Stones any more. **"**

Mick Jagger

"

We didn't even expect Brian to be there. If he turned up, we'd find something for him to do. I'd ask him, 'You got anything?' You know, 'What do you think about this? Want to put something over this?' But by then, he was already in Bye-Bye Land. "

Keith Richards on Brian Jones

"

At some point in every show, you just lose it. You get such interaction with the audience that it feels really good. And it should be pushed. You should let yourself go. I mean, have those moments when you really are quite out of your brain.

Mick Jagger

"

"

I'm Sagittarius, half-man, half-horse, with a license to shit in the street.

Keith Richards

"

66

Sometimes I think, 'Oh, Jesus, do I really have to go on now?' **99**

Mick Jagger,
on touring

"

I've seen Keith fall asleep at business meetings about millions of dollars for him – because of heroin, just nod out and then wake up and answer a question. **"**

Charlie Watts

"

The idea of retiring is like killing yourself. It's almost like Harakiri. I intend to live to 100 and go down in history. **"**

Keith Richards

"

You can't accuse me of anything
I haven't already confessed to.

Keith Richards

"

❝

Keith still communicates through fax. That's why I never hear much from him – because I ain't got a fax machine. You get a message from Keith on a fax. You get, 'I don't know when, I don't know where, just get ready. Love, Keith.' **❞**

Ronnie Wood, 2011

"

I was listening to music long before rock 'n' roll.

"

Bill Wyman

66

I can't be left unsupervised.

Ronnie Wood

99

"

The Rolling Stones overtake you. And it's almost like you're sort of levitating. You don't even want to touch the strings 'cause they're doing it themselves. And, any way, they'd be too hot. **"**

Keith Richards

"

To me, the real interest in playing guitar is to play guitar with another guy. Two guitars together, if you get it right, it can become like an orchestra.

"

Keith Richards

"

Brian could be the sweetest, softest, most considerate man in the world and the nastiest piece of work you've ever met. **"**

Bill Wyman

"

Andrew Oldham, went around London and he heard we were kicking up a storm in some clubs. He took a look around and he said, 'Hey, there can't be just one band in England.'

"

Keith Richards,
on Andrew Oldham

"

Brian was the first person I ever heard playing slide electric guitar. Mick and I both thought he was incredible.

"

**Keith Richards,
on Brian Jones**

"

Poor old cockroaches.

"

Keith Richards,
when told only he and cockroaches
would survive a nuclear holocaust

"

To be honest, he was a bit of a bastard. And it doesn't surprise me that he came to a sticky end. **"**

**Keith Richards,
on Brian Jones**

CHAPTER

FOUR

PRODIGAL
SONS

"

With Mick, it was basically music. We had been playmates — we happened to go to the same school for a while. But it was me seeing him again on the train, as a teenager, with the blues records, that was the bombshell — to suddenly find we were both madly in love with the blues, churning to get to the bottom of this thing. **"**

Keith Richards

"

Mick Jagger is the perfect rock star. There's nobody more perfect than Jagger. He's rude, he's ugly-attractive, he's brilliant. The Rolling Stones are the perfect rock group – they don't give a fuck. **"**

Elton John

"

I didn't have any inhibitions. I saw Elvis and Gene Vincent, and I thought, 'Well, I can do this'. And I liked doing it. It's a real buzz, even in front of 20 people, to make a complete fool of yourself. **"**

Mick Jagger

"

I thought it was ludicrous to take one of those gongs from the Establishment… it's not what the Stones is about, is it? I don't want to step out on stage with someone wearing a fucking coronet and sporting the old ermine. I told Mick, 'It's a fucking paltry honour.' **"**

Keith Richards,
on Mick's knighthood, 2003

"

Brian Jones had a death wish at a young age. Brian's talent wasn't up to it. He wasn't up to leading a band. He was not a pleasant person to be around. And he was never there to help people to write a song. That's when Mick lost his patience. We carried Brian Jones.

"

Charlie Watts

"

There's something beautifully friendly and elevating about a bunch of guys playing music together. This wonderful little world that is unassailable. It's really teamwork, one guy supporting the others, and it's all for one purpose, and there's no flies in the ointment, for a while. And nobody conducting, it's all up to you.

"

Keith Richards

"

If I wanted to hear the essence of Jagger and Richards together, I suppose it would be 'Midnight Rambler'. Anybody else could have written any of our other songs; but, I don't think anybody could have written 'Midnight Rambler' except Mick and me. And nobody else would have thought of making an opera out of the blues. **"**

Keith Richards, 2012

66

Maybe I thought that I would be able to protect my family from – not Keith's orbit – but, drugs. Because, I slowly became addicted to heroin. There comes a point where you have to choose between one or the other or you die. And I, you know, I survived.

Mick Taylor, 2012

"

Rock and roll ain't nothing but jazz
with a hard backbeat. **"**

Keith Richards

"

When people talk about the '60s, I never think that was me there. It was me and I was in it, but I was never enamoured with all that. It's supposed to be sex and drugs and rock and roll and I'm not really like that. I've never really seen the Rolling Stones as anything. **"**

Charlie Watts

"

After food, air, water and warmth, music is the next necessity of life.

Keith Richards

"

My mother has always been unhappy with what I do. She would rather I do something nicer, like be a bricklayer. "

Mick Jagger

> **"** We were young, good-looking and stupid. Now we're just stupid. **"**

Mick Jagger,
on *Exile on Main Street*

"

Decadence is very enjoyable.

"

Mick Jagger

"

I'm not a musician, I just play bass.

Bill Wyman

"

"

I doubt he'd ever take anything that
would get the better of him. **"**

Mick Taylor,
on Mick Jagger's drug use

"

Having loved the Stones all the time I was growing up, I wasn't about to see them go and split up. It got very close to it in the '80s, when Mick thought that Keith hated him and vice versa.

"

Ronnie Wood

"

Give me a guitar, give me a piano, give me a broom and string, I wouldn't get bored anywhere. "

Keith Richards

"

The electric guitar was vital in helping what I've achieved – where would I be without it? Playing awfully quietly, for a start. **"**

Keith Richards

"

I'll say to Charlie, 'Should I go to Mick's room and hang him?', and he'll say, 'No.' His opinion counts.

Keith Richards

"

"

I'll kill you now, but your wife wouldn't like cleaning up your blood.

Ronnie Wood,
in an infamous argument with Keith

"

"

There's the sun, there's the moon, there's the air we breathe, and there's the Rolling Stones.   **"**

Keith Richards

"

We had a set of uniforms, but everybody kept losing his suit, so we decided to call it a day and go on as we like. **"**

Keith Richards

"

I could sit down with Mick Taylor, and he would play very fluid lines against my vocals. He was exciting, and he was very pretty, and it gave me something to follow, to bang off. Some people think that's the best version of the band that existed.

Mick Jagger

"

"

The thing about Brian [Jones] is that he was an extremely difficult person. He was very unhappy with life, very frustrated. He was very talented, but he was a very paranoid personality and not at all suited to be in show business. **"**

Mick Jagger

"

That was the final nail in the coffin with me and Brian. He'd never forgive me for that and I don't blame him, but hell, shit happens.

**Keith Richards,
on Anita Pallenberg, 2003**

"

CHAPTER

FIVE

**CAN'T
GET NO**

"

We do what we want to do. We write songs. We try not to repeat ourselves too much. We have our own sound and our own way of doing things. I wish that I could just sit in the audience for one night and see the show. Everyone in the band has said that at some point. But then you wouldn't be seeing the whole band. And that's the problem with that.

Keith Richards, 1974

"

"

'Satisfaction' echoed the thinking of any generation you care to name, including the present one. But we didn't set out on bits of paper that we were going to be the voice of a generation. The original aim of the Rolling Stones was to play blues. It wasn't even to play rock music.

Mick Jagger, 1987

"

It's kind of limiting using your intellect to write songs like 'Brown Sugar', isn't it? **"**

Mick Jagger

———————————————

"

I never would write that song now.

**Mick Jagger,
on 'Brown Sugar'**

"

———————————————

"

I've never had a problem with drugs.
I've had problems with the police.

Keith Richards

"

I'm not getting old – I'm evolving.

Keith Richards

"
A painter's got a canvas. The writer's got reams of empty paper. A musician has silence.

"

Keith Richards

"

I don't want to see my old friend Lucifer just yet. He's the guy I'm gonna see, isn't it? I'm not going to the Other Place, let's face it.

"

Keith Richards

"

I was totally comatose but I was totally awake. I could listen to everyone, and they were like, 'He's dead, he's dead!' waving their fingers and pushing me about, and I was thinking, 'I'm not dead!' **"**

Keith Richards

"

Everything was out of tune, sloppy,
but they had a chemistry that really
did come together on record.

Mick Taylor

"

"

It's all right leaping about the stage when you're 20 but when you get to 25 it gets a bit embarrassing.

Bill Wyman

"

If you don't know the blues...
there's no point in picking up the
guitar and playing rock and roll or
any other form of popular music.

Keith Richards

"

"

You see, to me, the art of music is listening to it, not playing it. The real art of it is hearing it. **"**

Keith Richards

"

I never plan anything, which is probably the difference between Mick and myself. Mick needs to know what he's gonna do tomorrow and I'm just happy to wake up to see who's hanging around. **"**

Keith Richards

"

Mick's rock and I'm roll.

Keith Richards

"

"

Sometimes I feel that my whole career with the Birds, Jeff Beck and the Faces was one long audition to join the Rolling Stones. I still think of myself as a fan as much as a band member.

"

Ronnie Wood, 2015

"

When you're about bad behaviour,
you start behaving badly. **"**

Keith Richards

"

I was under several indictments dotted all over the globe. But that was just my day-to-day life. **"**

Keith Richards,
of his 1970s drug busts, 2011

"

The reason Andrew Loog Oldham left was because he thought that we weren't concentrating and that we were being childish. It was not a great moment really – and I would have thought it wasn't a great moment for Andrew, either. There were a lot of distractions and you always need someone to focus you at that point – that was Andrew's job. **"**

Mick Jagger, 2003

"

When I first heard their stirring music coming from the tent at the Richmond Jazz and Blues festival in 1963, something happened inside me and I knew that was the band I wanted to be in. The thought of being in the Stones is what gave me the drive to carry on. "

Ronnie Wood, 2015

"

There is a change between material on *Satanic Majesties* and *Beggars Banquet*. I'd grown sick to death of the whole Maharishi guru shit and the beads and bells. Who knows where these things come from, but I guess [the music] was a reaction to what we'd done in our time off and also that severe dose of reality.

Keith Richards, 2003

"

"

A spell in prison will certainly give you room for thought… I was fucking pissed with being busted. So it was, 'Right, we'll go and strip this thing down.' There's a lot of anger in the music from that period. "

Keith Richards, 2003

"

When we got busted at Redlands, it suddenly made us realize that this was a whole different ball game and that was when the fun stopped. Up until then, it had been as though London existed in a beautiful space where you could do anything you wanted. **"**

Keith Richards, 2003

"

The thing that bugs me is that I get treated like the Grandfather of Pop, just like James Brown is regarded as the Grandfather of Soul. I don't know why we've kept going. I think really because we were successful.

Mick Jagger

"

It is all right letting yourself go, as long as you can get yourself back.

Keith Richards

"

"

It's hard to remember just what that period [the sixties] was like, but I can assure you it was extremely different from now. **"**

Mick Jagger

CHAPTER

SIX

THE GLIMMER
TWINS

"

Of course, I do occasionally arouse primeval instincts but, I mean, most men can do that. They can't do it to so many. I just happen to be able to do it to several thousand people. It's fun to do that. **"**

Mick Jagger

"

If you are going to get wasted, then get wasted elegantly.

,,

Keith Richards

"

I used to love Mick but I haven't been to his dressing room in 20 years. Sometimes I think: 'I miss my friend.' I wonder: 'Where did he go?'

Keith Richards

"

People have this obsession. They want you to be like you were in 1969. They want you to, because otherwise their youth goes with you. It's very selfish, but it's understandable. **"**

Mick Jagger

"

Some things get better with age.
Like me. **"**

Keith Richards

"

It's an overwhelming feeling, the audience. That must be why most of these people never give up performing. Because they just can't go without that sort of rush. It's a bit like having an orgasm. Sometimes an orgasm is better than being onstage; sometimes being onstage is better than an orgasm. **"**

Mick Jagger

66

It was the beginning of the eighties when Mick started to become unbearable. **99**

Keith Richards

"

As long as my face is on page one,
I don't care what they say about me
on page seventeen. **"**

Mick Jagger

"

Some doctor told me I had six months to live and I went to their funeral. **"**

Keith Richards

"

Mick has a tiny todger. I know he's got an enormous pair of balls but it doesn't quite fill the gap.   "

Keith Richards, 2007

"

Either we stay at home and become pillars of the community or we go out and tour. We couldn't really find any communities that still needed pillars. **"**

Mick Jagger

"

Quite honestly, you're probably in a den of madmen. For some weird reason, we've been given an extra leash. **"**

Keith Richards

"

I have never wanted to give up performing on stage, but one day the tours will be over. **"**

Mick Jagger

___

"

I've been through more cold turkeys
than there are freezers. **"**

Keith Richards

___

"

This is a concept most people who run rock-'n'-roll tours can't grasp – what's the point of spending a year touring and earning no money when you could be back in America, earning money. **"**

Mick Jagger

"

If you're going to kick authority in the teeth, you might as well use two feet. **"**

Keith Richards

66

Drinking and taking drugs and having
sex. It was just part of life. It wasn't
really anything special. It was just a
bit of a bore, really. Everyone took
drugs the whole time, and you were
out of it the whole time. It wasn't a
special event. **99**

Mick Jagger

"
The Stones might not last forever but we'll be going until sometime this side of ever. **"**

Mick Jagger

Fame has killed more very talented guys than drugs.

Keith Richards

"

If you've gotta think about being cool, you ain't cool. **"**

Keith Richards

"

My parents were extremely disapproving of it all. Because it was just not done. This was for very low-class people, remember. Rock-'n'-roll singers weren't educated people.

Mick Jagger

"

"

I was Number One on the 'Who's Likely to Die' list for ten years… I was really disappointed when I fell off that list. **"**

Keith Richards

"

Rock and roll is a spent force. It is merely recycling itself and everything is a rehash of something else. I'm not that good a musician to break out of it – it's all I can do.

Mick Jagger

"

There's a demon in me, and he's still around. Without the dope, we have a bit more of a chat these days.

Keith Richards

"

Nobody wants to get old, but nobody wants to die young either.

Keith Richards

66

If only the whole world could stay young.

99

Mick Jagger

66

I had to stop doing Chuck Berry
and start doing Keith Richards.

Keith Richards

99

"

You realize that these girls are going, either quietly or loudly, sort of crazy [for you]. And you're going, 'Well, this is good.' **"**

Mick Jagger,
on girl fans

66

You know the British Museum has one of those glass cases with my liver's name on it… and they're going to have to wait a fucking long time.

99

Keith Richards

"

There's not many Americans, certainly not many of the teenagers I met when I first went to America, knew anything about blues musicians at all. They do now, which is very groovy. **"**

Mick Jagger, 1968

"

There have been great studies in medical science lately. That's why I am able to say to you, 'Good evening, ladies and gentleman. Welcome to the Rock and Roll Hall of Fame.'

Keith Richards

"

"

America's obviously changed since we first came here. It's almost unrecognizable and it's very hard to imagine what the United States was like 40 years ago. We've definitely grown with the American culture changes. "

Mick Jagger

"

Do you think when we get together we're all like happy families? Forget about it. We've been fighting cats and dogs all our career. **"**

Keith Richards,
on Mick, 2011

"

When I was 18 or so, the Rolling Stones were just starting to play some clubs around London, and I realized I was getting a lot of girl action when normally I hadn't gotten much. I was very unsophisticated then. **"**

Mick Jagger

"

I don't encourage anybody to do what I do, you know? Why should you? More for me! **"**

Keith Richards, 2006

"

To go from the music-oriented press to national press and national television, and everyone seeing you in the world of two television channels, and then being recognized by everyone from builders and people working in shops and so on. It goes to your head – very champagne-feeling. "

Mick Jagger

"

I'm all for a quiet life. I just didn't get one. **"**

Keith Richards